REFLECTIONS AT HOME
The Morning
Star Series

REFLECTIONS AT HOME
The Morning
Star Series

Relevant Daily Scriptures For the Informed Christian

FEBRUARY WORKBOOK

CRYSTAL V. HENRY

authorHOUSE®

AuthorHouse™
1663 Liberty Drive
Bloomington, IN 47403
www.authorhouse.com
Phone: 1-800-839-8640

Published by AuthorHouse   05/23/2012

ISBN: 978-1-4772-0746-8 (sc)
ISBN: 978-1-4772-0745-1 (e)

Library of Congress Control Number: 2011960206

Any people depicted in stock imagery provided by Thinkstock are models, and such images are being used for illustrative purposes only.
Certain stock imagery © Thinkstock.

This book is printed on acid-free paper.

Because of the dynamic nature of the Internet, any web addresses or links contained in this book may have changed since publication and may no longer be valid. The views expressed in this work are solely those of the author and do not necessarily reflect the views of the publisher, and the publisher hereby disclaims any responsibility for them.

**This workbook is dedicated to Allen &
Gwendolyn Foster who taught my soul to sing.**

REFLECTIONS AT HOME

PREFACE

In today's climate of campaign adversity, there are those who use hatred and race to win over a unique set of people who claim to be Christians, yet whose actions are an abomination to God. The four Gospels—Matthew, Mark, Luke, and John—all tell us about the life of Jesus but each from a different perspective. I believe the Founding Fathers were thinking of this when they wrote "out of many, one" comparing the Constitution to the Gospels which teaches us unity and diversity. As you read the daily scriptures more and more until it becomes a part of your daily routine, you will discover that the first three Gospels—Matthew, Mark and Luke—are known as the Synoptic Gospels. They speak of the life of Jesus in a similar manner using parables and epigrams whereas the Gospel of John is written in a different style using long speeches and dialogue explaining the significance of Jesus' words.

Just as this book will make the reader cognizant of the times in which we live, the Gospels as Historical Literature tell us of the traditions of a people and serve as a source of information to increase our own understanding. The Gospels are also seen as Narrative Literature and teaches us through the use of story-telling such as "Dave and the Giant Pickle" in the Veggie Tales animated series. Last, the Gospels are seen as Theological Literature because they teach us how we should live and encourage those who believe. This is how I know that race-baiting dialogue in politics, or anywhere else is wrong and should not be accepted, especially by all who claim to be devout Christians, with a dismissive wave of the hand and a chuckle of tolerance and denial before going to a commercial. How do we explain to our children who hear this divisive rhetoric day after day and see Black political analyst making excuses for those who slander their own race, whether it be "Food Stamps President", or "making sure the Blacks on welfare don't get any of the hard-working White people's money"? As the Narrative genre suggests, I explain this oddity to my grandchildren that people who defend their would-be oppressors have been drinking the magical milk of the white cows of Ireland.

JANUARY REVIEW

1. Who said, "**Changes and** war are ever with me"? (Jan. 3)
2. What does the peacock symbolize? (Jan. 5)
3. What prophet was placed in stocks? (Jan. 6)
4. Antiochus IX ordered the Jews to worship whom? (Jan. 9)
5. What was the rededication of the Jewish temple in Jerusalem called? (Jan. 11)
6. Where is the Republic of Burundi located? (Jan. 12)
7. What is apostasy? (Jan. 14)
8. Who was the first Black physician in Jacksonville, Florida? (Jan. 17)
9. Flies consume only what kind of food? (Jan. 23)
10. Osceola was from which tribe? (Jan. 25)

FEBRUARY 1st

REFLECTIONS AT HOME
EZEKIEL 23: 1-4

". . . the Assyrians conquered Palestine's northern kingdom. The victors captured a large number of Israelites as slaves. Those who remained intermarried with the new Assyrian colonists."

from *The Damascus Way*
by Bunn & Oke

THE RAINBOW

Has there been a time when you thought yourself superior to someone else? Why? Was it because of where you were born? Was it because of the college you attended? Was it because of a physical feature you possess that is idealized by society? In this allegory, Jerusalem is warned about feeling superior to her sister city, Samaria. I have found that many times in life, people feel superior to others when they have had no personal relationship outside of their own culture.

As we learned in the January workbook, Amos was charged by God to travel and warn the wealthy not to ignore the poor. In *Damascus Way*, not until Jamal, the Syrian trader; Julia, daughter of a Samarian: Linux, the Roman legion; and the Ethiopian traveled from their place of origin, did they find the commonality of mankind. I recently traveled to beautiful Strousbourg, France and Heidleburg, Germany where the cobblestone streets and quaint shops were like going back in time. As we meandered beneath the multitude of cascading flowers in carefully arranged flower boxes, we saw that as with the flowers, the people made up a living quilt.

It made me think of Stoudtburg Village in Adamstown, PA. The village tries to give one the same feeling as walking through the European hamlets of yesteryear. The major difference is the lack of a mixture of cultures. I have a friend named Simpson, who is a gifted artist and would be a fantastic asset as well as bring something missing to the makeup of the Village. For those people of various ancestry, I encourage you to not only visit or become a merchant of Stoudtburg, but consider moving to Adamstown (an hour from Philadelphia) to own a home away from the big city.

When people live together, they get to form relationships, and a sense of community develops allowing myths, untruths, and old prejudices to die.

"Jesus and the Woman of Samaria" *by Gustave Doré*

Doré Bible Illustrations • Free to Copy www. creationism.org/images/

Job 4:13-14 Jesus answered and said unto her, Whosoever drinketh of this water shall thirst again; But whosoever drinketh of the water that I shall give him shall never thirst: . . . .

ALLEGORY

A STORY IN WHICH THE CHARACTERS AND THE SETTING STAND FOR ABSTRACT IDEAS AND MORAL QUALITIES

NATIONAL BLACK HISTORY MONTH

FEBRUARY 1ST

CONGRATULATIONS TO THE 44th PRESIDENT OF THE UNITED STATES, BARACK HUSSEIN OBAMA.

Still I Rise

You may write me down in history
With your bitter, twisted lies,
You may trod me in the very dirt
But still, like dust, I'll rise.

Does my sassiness upset you?
Why are you beset with gloom?
'Cause I walk like I've got oil wells
Pumping in my living room.

Just like moons and the suns,
With the certainty of tides,
Just like hopes springing high,
Still I'll rise.

Did you want to see me broken?
Bowed head and lowered eyes?
Shoulders falling down like teardrops,
Weakened by my soulful cries.

Does my haughtiness offend you?
Don't you take it awful hard
'Cause I laugh like I've got gold mines
Diggin' in my own back yard.

You may shoot me with your words,
You may cut me with your eyes,
You may kill me with your hatefulness,
But still, like air, I'll rise.

Does my sexiness upset you?
Does it come as a surprise
That I dance like I've got diamonds
At the meeting of my thighs?

Out of the huts of history's shame
I rise
Up from a past that's rooted in pain
I rise
I'm a black ocean, leaping and wide,
Welling and swelling I bear in the tide.
Leaving behind nights of terror and fear
I rise
Into a daybreak that's wondrously clear
I rise
Bringing the gifts that my ancestors gave,
I am the dream and the hope of the slave,
I rise
I rise
I rise.

Maya Angelou

FEBRUARY 2ND

REFLECTIONS AT HOME
2 SAMUEL 21: 15-22

BLIND LOYALTY

There are times in life when someone is so loyal to a cause or person, he acts before thinking. This behavior is especially destructive when done en masse such as with the current Republican in Congress known as the "Do-Nothing" Congress. Some have even signed pledges, as if running the country can take a stoic point of view, ignoring the common man of the day.

This was the plight of Abishai who truly was devoted to David, however it is not enough to be physically strong to defeat the Philistine giants of today. True leaders must be wise and have self-control. Former presidents have never had to endure the arrogant racist antics of a bony, age-spotted finger being wagged in their faces, or a Supreme Court Justice mouthing "that's not true" as the President warns the nation that by allowing undisclosed millions of dollars to be poured into the election process, it would lead to distorting the outcome, or the disrespectful shout of "you lie" by an average Joe. While visiting in Germany, someone said to me "It's like the Ku Klux Klan has taken over the Republican Party." Europeans know the history of our country better than some candidates who are running for the highest office in the land, as the news anchors dance around the pole of political correctness.

Like Abishai, who was usually under the command of his younger brother, Joab, the Tea Party of 2011 seem to be dictating commands to the Speaker of the House. Congress has given the appearance of a trailer full of hypocrites, racists, and liars that will destroy this country out of blind loyalty to what? The Confederate Flag? Power? Greed? The concept of millionaires paying their fair share is abhorrent to many in Congress because they would be voting against themselves.

It is your responsibility to learn of the character of those you elect to office. Visit the CREW (Citizens for Responsibility & Ethics in Washington) website *www.crewsmostcorrupt.org* and research why Rep. Vern Buchanan; David Vitter; Joe Walsh; Eric Canter; Anthony Weiner; Charles Bass; and many more are mentioned and judge for yourself. You cannot afford to be a victim of blind loyalty.

"Abishai Saves the Life of David" *by Gustave Doré*

Doré Bible Illustrations
• Free to Copy www.
creationism.org/images/

2Sa 21:17 But Abishai . . . smote the Philistine, and killed him. Then the men of David sware unto him, saying, Thou shalt go no more out with us to battle, that thou quench not the light of Israel.

NATIONAL BLACK HISTORY MONTH

FEBRUARY 2nd

**PRESIDENT OBAMA SUPPORTS
"THE DREAM ACT"
(DEVELOPMENT, RELIEF, AND
EDUCATION FOR ALIEN MINORS)
WHICH IS DESIGNED TO PROVIDE
CONDITIONAL PERMANENT RESIDENCY
FOR THOSE WHO ARRIVED IN THE U.S.
AS CHILDREN**

FEBRUARY 3RD

REFLECTIONS AT HOME
2 CORINTHIANS 11: 1-15

THE HIRAGASY

There are times in life when someone will have a "calling". This usually means that there is something within which drives an unexplainable passion for a cause. Usually, this desire is not what the individual has had in the way of formal training. Notice that I said "formal" training indicating school. Yet, such a person has trained himself by reading and studying, or working with people who share the same passion. Such was the dilemma of Paul. Scholars of his day were usually trained in Greek schools of oratory. In fact, professional reciters of poetry (which was an occupation) were called rhapsodes.

During the time of Paul there existed a doctrine known as Gnosticism. This was a belief that spiritual knowledge, rather than faith, was essential to salvation. Paul preached that the content of what he was saying outweighed his presentation, which probably did not have the grandiose of other scholars. He reminded the people that they should be more concerned with the lifestyle of the "teacher". Was it consistent with Biblical morality or more of a self-serving or pagan deity? The amount charged by the spiritual teachers did not always indicate their true worth, for Paul charged nothing.

Even today, there are persons who because of their occupation, should be excellent communicators. However, like Paul, the skill of an orator does not come easily. There is a musical tradition in Madagascar,

Africa which is known as hiragasy. During the 18th century, the people first used musicians to draw a crowd to make political speeches, and to communicate information to the various villages. This is called kabary. Musicians often used their dances and songs as a means of criticizing their French rulers. We are familiar with how the American slave used music as well in the form of spirituals as a code language to outsmart their oppressors. During the French colonial period of Madagascar, such musicians were often exempt from the usual forced labor requirements of their oppressors.

If you have a "calling" like Paul, do not let your lack of formal education stop you. If you can not afford college to become a veterinarian, then volunteer at an animal shelter or start an annual Rhapsode Contest for high school students and adults at your church. There is a wonderful organization called "Poetry Out Loud" you can contact on its website.

"St. Paul Preaching to the Thessalonians" *by Gustave Doré*

Doré Bible Illustrations
• Free to Copy www.
creationism.org/images/

1Th 2:11-12 As ye know how we exhorted and comforted and charged everyone of you, as a father *doth* his children, That ye would walk worthy of God, who hath called you unto his kingdom and glory.

NATIONAL BLACK HISTORY MONTH

FEBRUARY 3RD

PRESIDENT OBAMA SIGNED INTO LAW THE "FY2010 NATIONAL DEFENSE AUTHORIZATION ACT" WHICH INCLUDED THE MATTHEW SHEPARD & JAMES BYRD, JR. HATE CRIMES PREVENTION ACT.

FEBRUARY 4TH

REFLECTIONS AT HOME
ACTS 6: 8-15

FACES OF THE LIBERTINES

In April of 1945, one hundred sixty-two African American officers in the United States Army Air Force on the 477th Bombardment Group were arrested for protesting the segregation of officer club facilities. This was known as the Freeman Field Mutiny in Indiana. I remember how my father hated the military's treatment of Black families. The Black wives had to ride in the filthy caboose of the trains taking them to meet their husbands returning from WWII, while the Caucasian wives rode in the clean, comfortable seats in the front cars. It was no better for the returning soldiers. The Black soldiers had to ride in the same dirty caboose cars while the Nazi prisoners rode comfortably in the front cars. How my ancestors endured this form of American "freedom" makes me respect them even more for their wisdom and strength to last so that my generation would not have to suffer the law of the land.

The evangelist, Stephen, who was selected by the apostles to help organize the followers of Jesus was wrongly accused of preaching against Moses' laws found in the Pentateuch or Torah. These are the first five books in the Bible, from Genesis to Deuteronomy. The Libertines, also known as Freedmen (a group of Jewish slaves who had been freed by Rome) seemed to have adapted to the mindscape of their oppressors. They turned the people against Stephen by spreading lies, they set up

14

false witnesses, and they finally caused his arrest. Sound familiar? Today, we would say that he was "swift-boated".

When the laws of a country mistreat its citizens through its actions, it changes the fabric of all of its citizens. No one had a problem with men sent to Italy and Africa to fight, yet these same Black soldiers could not stay in a hotel in the Southern states. Likewise, no one came to rescue or rebuke the false allegations against Stephen. In Oscar Wilde's novel, *Dorian Gray*, every time he committed a sinful act, his handsome portrait became more grotesque. Apathy and sin have a way of working from within a person. In your lifetime, how many different faces have you worn? What do others see in your face? Does your face portray something evil or do others look at you and see the face of an angel?

Freeman Field Mutiny

http://en.wikipedia.org/wiki/File:Freeman_Field_Mutiny.jpg

"Martydom of St. Stephen" *by Gustave Doré*

Doré Bible Illustrations
• Free to Copy www.
creationism.org/images/

Act 7:59-60 And they stoned Stephen, calling upon *God*, and saying, Lord Jesus, receive my spirit. . . . Lord, lay not this sin to their charge. And when he had said this, he fell asleep.

16

NATIONAL BLACK HISTORY MONTH

FEBRUARY 4TH

PRESIDENT OBAMA RATIFIED A LANDMARK NUCLEAR ARMS TREATY WITH RUSSIA KNOWN AS "NEW START".

FEBRUARY 5TH

REFLECTIONS AT HOME
MARK 6: 1-6

ISN'T HE THE CARPENTER?

Unfortunately some people will only see you as who you used to be and not as who you are today. This passage tells us that many times these people are your family and friends. The very ones who you look to for support and encouragement, are the ones who refuse to see the growth and possibilities God has given to you in the form of opportunities because He allows free choice. What you decide to do with your creativity is up to you.

These preconceived notions and prejudices may be grounded in jealousy, and lack of faith in the person they remembered as a youth. When Jesus left Nazareth and returned with the disciples, the people of the village still saw him as only the son of the carpenter named Joseph. Because they refused to accept Jesus for whom He had become, He chose not to perform all of the miracles He could have done.

"And He marveled because of their unbelief." (Verse 6:6)

There is a statue in front of the Philadelphia City Hall of a man named Matthias W. Baldwin. In the 1800's, he owned one of the most successful locomotive manufacturing firms in America. However, this New Jersey native lost his father at the age of four and was one of five children. At the age of sixteen, he was apprenticed to learn how to make jewelry. By age twenty-four, he had devised a patent for gold plating. Baldwin then went on to open a printing shop which was powered by his self-designed steam engine. By age thirty-six, he built his first locomotive which grew to some fifteen hundred steam locomotives before his death in 1866.

Because this young man who once designed jewelry understood what is was like to have access to opportunity, Baldwin donated money to build a school for African-American children in Philadelphia and supported the movement to allow Black men to vote as well as supported the abolitionist movement. His choice to follow the teachings of Jesus rather than the reasoning of racists, led to a boycott of Baldwin locomotives by railroads in the Southern states. And even today, we marvel at their unbelief that all men are created equal.

"Jesus Healing the Sick" *by Gustave Doré*

Doré Bible Illustrations
• Free to Copy www.
creationism.org/images/

Mat 15:31 Insomuch that the multitude wondered, when they saw the dumb to speak, the maimed to be whole, the lame to walk, and the blind to see: and they glorified the God of Israel.

20

NATIONAL BLACK HISTORY MONTH

FEBRUARY 5TH

PRESIDENT OBAMA ANNOUNCED THE CREATION OF A "JOINT VIRTUAL LIFETIME ELECTRONIC RECORD" FOR MEMBERS OF THE U.S. ARMED FORCES TO IMPROVE THE QUALITY OF MEDICAL CARE

FEBRUARY 6TH

REFLECTIONS AT HOME
AMOS 2: 6-16

THE WARNING

God condemned Israel for many things: exploiting the poor, worshiping false gods such as money, and taking illegal collateral for loans to name a few. Their response to those in need was one of arrogance and greed. He warns about bribing court officials as some say is a serious problem that we face today on the Supreme Court as judges are serenaded at parties given by political advocates. Nazarites took a vow of service to abstain from wine and to never cut their hair. The radical Congress has also taken a vow whereby the country be damned as they serve the masters of their purse strings. God's law is more concerned with doing what is right. He warns that the actions of the Nazarites will be punished.

There is a need for representatives of the common man. Although President Obama has had to endure the hypocrites who deliberately block everything and anything that benefits the middle class, perhaps he should just say the heck with them and press on as President Roosevelt did in the 1930's when he knew that he had to address the plight of the disfranchisement of African Americans. In 1935, President and Mrs. Roosevelt established the "Black Cabinet", known as the Federal Council of Negro Affairs to advise him on public policy. One of the forty-five members of this council was Mary McLeon Bethune, a civil rights leader and educator.

The arrogant people who call the "Occupy Wall Street" a mob, yet saw the hate-filled racists in the Republican Tea Party who carried signs of President Obama as Hitler and monkeys, and who spat on Black Congressmen were said to be "grass root organizations" by Cantor and crew.

Can you name forty-five people who could comprise a minority policy advisory committee today? Fill in your suggestions on the next page.

Remember, it was the Senators that stabbed Julius Caesar in the name of "saving" the Republic. But, as today, they ignored the will of the people and were later defeated at the Battle of Philippi in 42BC. Perhaps it is time once again to defeat the Senators along with Blue Dog Democrats by sending them home to join the ranks of the unemployed.

MINORITY CABINET OF 2012

1. Joy-Ann Reid—managing editor, *www.grio.com*
2. Karen Hunter—journalist
3. Martin Bashir—MSNBC Anchor
4. Earl Ofari Hutchinson—author
5. Joe Madison—civil rights activist
6. Michael Eric Dyson, PhD—professor of sociology at Georgetown U.
7. Obery Hendricks, PhD—professor of Biblical Interpretation at NY Theological Seminary
8. Goldie Taylor—political analyst
9. Russell Simmons—music producer
10. Renee C. Hughes—former Common Pleas Court Judge, CEO
11. Rev. Marvin E. Wiley—Rock of Ages Baptist Church in Illinois
12. Melissa Harris-Perry—MSNBC anchor, Prof. At Tulane U.
13. Neil D. Tyson, PhD—astrophysicist, director of Hayden Planetarium
14. James Peterson, PhD—director of Africana Studies at Lehigh U.
15. Heather McGhee—journalist, *www.demos.org*
16. Richard Kim—journalist, *www.thenation.com*
17. Marshall P. Mitchell—marketing, *www.differentdrummer.com*
18. Dr. Gerald DeVaughn—cardiologist
19. Rev. Al Sharpton—MSNBC anchor, civil rights activist
20. Tyler Perry—movie mogul
21. _____
22. _____
23. _____
24. _____
25. _____

26. _____

27. _____

28. _____

29. _____

30. _____

31. _____

32. _____

33. _____

34. _____

35. _____

36. _____

37. _____

38. _____

39. _____

40. _____

41. _____

42. _____

43. _____

44. _____

45. _____

Daytona School with Bethune

http://en.wikipedia.org/wiki/
File:Daytona_School_with_Bethune . . .

"Amos" *by Gustave Doré*

Amos 12 The words of Amos, who was among the herdmen of Tekoa, which he saw concerning Israel in the days of Uzziah king of Judah, . . . two years before the earthquake.

NATIONAL BLACK HISTORY MONTH

FEBRUARY 6TH

PRESIDENT OBAMA SIGNED THE "FAIR SENTENCING ACT" WHICH REDUCED THE DISPARITY IN THE AMOUNTS OF POWDER COCAINE (GENERALLY USED BY WHITES), AND CRACK COCAINE (GENERALLY USED BY BLACKS)

FEBRUARY 7TH

REFLECTIONS AT HOME
JEREMIAH 46: 1-12

"CRYSTAL TRESSES"

In ancient times, comets streaming across the midnight sky signified a change of times was about to happen. Shakespeare referred to the shining tails of the comet as "crystal tresses".

In today's verses, the Lord is seen here as a warrior who will come to give judgement on all who have lived their lives filled with prejudice and preclusive tactics instead of fairness and justice. Jeremiah was sent to deliver the message that all who are hypocrites and self-serving will face judgement one day. Down the road and around the corner, judgement comes to all.

So, when one reads the website of millionaire Congressman Michael McCaul of Texas, the contradictions are glaring. He claims to hold hearings to investigate aspects of "waste, fraud, and abuse." Being an integral part of the Republican do-nothing Congress, some say the salary he receives for obstruction has been a major waste. McCaul co-authored a report concerning Homeland Security called "A Line in the Sand . . .", yet has not shown any integrity to even give President Obama a word of credit for the extraordinary judgement and courage displayed in the killing of Bin Laden and other terrorists.

If a lie is repeated often enough, the ignorant masses will believe it. Is this why many of the hypocritical Congressmen who voted against the President's stimulus bill, were secretly begging for the money and taking credit for the jobs it produced? For millionaires like McCaul who married Linda, a millionaire in her own right as the daughter of Clear Channel Communications and sister to the CEO, the 2.9 million jobs created by the stimulus plan seemed like peanuts, but not to those newly hired. To those like McCaul who received nearly $300 million a year, it was a "failure". Using this same jaded point of view, McCaul voted to stop federal funding of National Public Radio. After all, you can listen to Clear Channel.

So, Congressman Michael McCaul must be one of those "job creators". It would really be wonderful if he would hire twelve graduates of Wiley College to put his money where his mouth is so to speak. Wiley is famous for its great debate teams as seen in the movie starring Denzel Washington. As the Christian he claims to be, he knows that one day he will have to account for turning a blind eye and a deaf ear to the needs of the poor when he was given a position to help those less fortunate and did nothing! Republicans have voted against fuel assistance, the Clean Air Act, and food stamps on which many rely. In God we trust!

"Jeremiah" *by Gustave Doré*

Doré Bible Illustrations
• Free to Copy www. creationism.org/images/

Jer 1:14-15 Then the Lord said unto me, Out of the north an evil shall break forth . . . and they shall come, and they shall set every one his throne at the entering of the gates of Jerusalem . . . .

NATIONAL BLACK HISTORY MONTH

FEBRUARY 7TH

PRESIDENT OBAMA SIGNED INTO LAW THE "AFFORDABLE CARE ACT (ACA)" WHICH ESTABLISHES THE "COMMUNITY LIVING ASSISTANCE SERVICES AND SUPPORTS" (CLASS), A SELF-FUNDED AND VOLUNTARY LONG-TERM CARE INSURANCE CHOICE THAT WOULD HELP PEOPLE WITH DISABILITIES REMAIN IN THEIR HOMES, COMMUNITIES AND JOBS THROUGH CASH BENEFITS TO PAY FOR COMMUNITY SUPPORT SERVICES

FEBRUARY 8TH

REFLECTIONS AT HOME
NEHEMIAH 4: 1-10

COMPLETING THE TASK

As the official cupbearer to the Persian king, Artaxerxes, Nehemiah had little power, but great influence. Because of this, he was allowed to return to Jerusalem to do something about the rebuilding of the city walls. For many of us who literally grew up in the church, to see the church crumble before your eyes due to various circumstances, breaks one heart. So, I understand how Nehemiah felt the need to do something. Since he was not the official leader of the church, he was ridiculed by Tobiah and his "yes men" in the attempt to discourage and sow the seed of doubt in the impossibility of rebuilding. But, in spite of the expected defeat on his part, Nehemiah responded to the teasing by praying and planning. With those who had not forgotten their glorious past, as people often do, they rebuilt the wall in fifty-two days.

Such was the life of two fabulous women I like to call "The Cochran Girls". Nellie Bly was a famous journalist in the 1800's, but was perhaps most famous for her pretending to be insane to expose the treatment of women at the Women's Lunatic Asylum for the "New York World" newspaper which was owned by Joseph Pulitzer. To learn more of this crusader whose real name was Elizabeth Jane Cochran, read her book *Ten Days in a Mad-House*. I even heard a song this week on NPR radio, (you know, the one Congressman McCaul voted to stop funding) called "Nellie Bly" by Stephen Foster.

Another pioneer in the face of opposition was Jacqueline Cochran, born Bessie Lee Pittman. One of five children in Alabama, she married very young as many did to escape a disagreeable life, but tragedy followed her to Florida where her five-year old son set his clothes afire while playing in the backyard unattended. After the accident, Jackie held various jobs as a hairdresser and even worked for awhile at Saks Fifth Avenue until she met millionaire Floyd Odlum. She began to take flying lessons and with Odlum's help, she established her own cosmetics line called "Wings", and flew her own aircraft promoting the line.

She and Amelia Earhart pioneered the way for female flight. Jacqueline Cochran not only helped to take American planes to Britain before the U.S. entered WWII, she was the first woman to fly a bomber across the Atlantic, and the first woman to break the sound barrier. If you think you might want a chance to fly, first pray about it; then study the history of the Women Airforce Service Pilots known as WASP as part of your preparation; then plan to go see an Air Force recruiter. Complete the task given to you.

"Nehemiah Viewing Secretly the Ruins of the Walls of Jerusalem" *by Gustave Doré*

Doré Bible Illustrations
• Free to Copy www. creationism.org/images/

Neh 2:13 And I went out by night by the gate of the valley, even before the dragon well, and to the dung port, and viewed the walls of Jerusalem, which were broken down, and the gates thereof were consumed with fire.

Many times you may feel that you have opposition all around you as Nehemiah felt. Sometimes understanding the motives of those who ridicule you, makes them less a threat whether it be jealousy, wealth, or fame. Using the semantic map below, research the motives of each of his detractors, then write a paragraph (5 sentences) for each group forming an essay. If need be, the same can be done with your name in the middle.

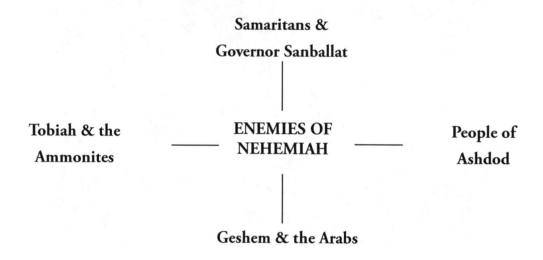

Nellie Bly journalist

http://en.wikipedia.org/wiki/File:Nellie_Bly_journalist.jpg

NATIONAL BLACK HISTORY MONTH

FEBRUARY 8TH

PRESIDENT OBAMA SIGNED THE LILLY LEDBETTER FAIR PAY ACT, RESTORING BASIC PROTECTIONS AGAINST PAY DISCRIMINATION FOR WOMEN

FEBRUARY 9TH

REFLECTIONS AT HOME
JOHN 14: 1-14

FIND A WAY

On this day, I reflect on an earthly angel named Mia Farrow. Having a famous actress for a mother, Maureen O'Sullivan, Mia always seemed to be a humble person. After having four biological children, Mia adopted eleven additional children from all over the world. Most people know of this, but they do not know that she also worked with the "Dream for Darfur" organization, or with "UNICEF" as the goodwill ambassador, or with the "United Buddy Bears" program out of Berlin. This was her way to "consider the least of these".

You've heard of composers like Beethoven, who lost the ability to hear but could still write beautiful music because they could still hear it within. Has music ever soothed your sorrow? Made your heart lighter? At a funeral the pastor would say "I am the way, the truth, and the life. No one comes to the Father except through Me" acknowledging that a loved one is making a necessary journey for now, but then I would hear the voice of Cleola singing "Let Not Your Heart Be Troubled" or the Wilberforce University Choir singing "In My Father's House Are Many Mansions" and while the women hold the note on "so-o-o-o" for what seems like forever, Maestro Jeremy Winston directs the alto, tenor and bass in a Gregorian-like chant to repeat the refrain each time softer than the last, "If it were not so, I would have told you." My God, my God.

When He sends his angels to sing, you have to believe. Sometimes music that touches one's soul is the way.

"And if I go and prepare a place for you, I will come again, and receive you unto myself . . ." (Verse 3)

♪

Plan a family movie night: FOUR DECADES OF A PHILANTHROPIST—MIA FARROW

"Rosemary's Baby" (1968); "The Great Gatsby" (1974); "The Purple Rose of Cairo" (1985); and "Alice" (1990).

Kudos to you, Ms. Farrow and Happy Birthday!

NATIONAL BLACK HISTORY MONTH

FEBRUARY 9TH

PRESIDENT OBAMA REPEALED
"DON'T ASK, DON'T TELL"
SEPTEMBER 20, 2011

FEBRUARY 10TH

REFLECTIONS AT HOME
1 SAMUEL 2: 1-11

THE SONS OF HANNAH

Even though a woman can achieve financial security due to hard work and the passing of the Lilly Ledbetter Act assuring equal pay, sometimes she may still feel inadequate and even have doubts regarding her self-worth when she cannot bear a child. How many have prayed to God like Hannah for a son? In this prayer of thanks, Hannah's prayers were answered and as promised to God, she and her husband, Elkanah, brought their son Samuel to Eli, the priest, so that he could serve God.

As a mother of two children, I can only imagine the heartache of a barren woman who wants to carry a child that looks just like the man with whom she fell in love. However, I like to think that God, in His wisdom, knew that there would be so many children living without love, just waiting for someone to come along and give them a forever home.

Hannah Biddle was not quite as fortunate with her two sons. In the early 1800's, there was a place called "Bloody Island" in the Mississippi River which was the scene of many political duels. A man named Benton was accused of not having the right to vote because he hadn't paid his property tax and another named Brown, who favored emancipation, was challenged to a duel by T. Reynolds.

Similar to today, in the Panic of 1819, during a recession, the people blamed the Bank because of its credit policy of sitting on the money.

Nicholas Biddle was the president of the United States Bank in 1831. When someone named S. Pettis complained about Nicholas, his brother Thomas Biddle, challenged Pettis to a duel. They would up killing each other.

> "Talk no more so exceeding proudly; let not arrogancy come out of your mouth: for the Lord is a God of knowledge, and by him actions are weighed."

(Verse 3)

Take your sons to church where they can grow up learning about priorities, humility, and of the sacrifice of our Lord. Better sons make better husbands, who make better fathers.

"Samuel Blessing Saul" *by Gustave Doré*

Doré Bible Illustrations
• Free to Copy www.
creationism.org/images/

1Sa 9:21 And Saul answered and said, *Am* not I a Benjamite, of the smallest of the tribes of Israel? . . . wherefore then speakest thou so to me?

NATIONAL BLACK HISTORY MONTH

FEBRUARY 10TH

PRESIDENT OBAMA SIGNED INTO LAW THE REAUTHORIZATION OF THE "EARLY HEARING DETECTION AND INTERVENTION ACT", WHICH PROVIDES FUNDING FOR SCREENING, INTERVENTION, AND RESEARCH OF HEARING LOSS

FEBRUARY 11TH

REFLECTIONS AT HOME
PSALM 45: 1-17

A MANCINI MORNING

This psalm is known as a poem or love song for the occasion of the wedding of King Solomon, however when I read it I thought of one of the most gifted American composers that ever lived. At a time when the ignorant are taking music out of schools because they falsely claim there is no money, we'll never know what child has been musically touched by God. Raised in the steeltown of Aliquippa, PA, Enrico (Henry) was born to Italian immigrants who wound up in this harsh surrounding, but taught him to play the piccolo.

"Win victories for truth and mercy and justice" (45: 4)

Mancini was drafted into the Army in 1945 interrupting his study at the Juillard School of Music in New York, but in doing so, he was able to help liberate those in a German concentration camp. Still, he was able to return and create some of the most memorable songs ever written. One of my favorite songs he wrote is "Moon River" from the film *Breakfast at Tiffany's* starring Katherine Hepburn. You do not have to have a revolving half-million dollar credit account like Newt Gingrich to shop at Tiffany's. So, if you cannot afford "the pink panther", which is really a pink diamond, you can go online, and you'll see that Tiffany's has a very lovely selection of gifts for $150. and less. Buy a DVD of the movie from Amazon.com, get some pastry from a bakery (like Brown Betty Dessert

Boutique), and some coffee (I prefer Maxwell House Vanilla). On any given morning, just the two of you enjoy the movie, the food, and then give your significant other a small token of your love from Tiffany's when the movie ends. If you have children, when they return from the sitter, have a Pink Panther evening and show the hilarious antics of Inspector Clouseau. Let them make some pink cupcakes and strawberry milkshakes. It's important that you spend time with the children doing age-appropriate activities and that you always find the time to spend together without the children. When you hear Mancini, remember your special morning and smile.

"I will make your name to be remembered . . ." (45: 17)

To my husband: His eyes are darker than wine,
This humble soul, so devine.
Sometimes late, but right on time
Strong of build, strength of mind
So surreal, So sublime
God truly made him one of a kind
His eyes are darker than wine.

"Solomon Receiving the Queen of Sheba" *by Gustave Doré*

Doré Bible Illustrations
• Free to Copy www. creationism.org/images/

2Ch 9:1-2 And when the queen of Sheba heard of the fame of Solomon, she came to prove Solomon with hard questions at Jerusalem, . . . And Solomon told her all her questions . . . .

NATIONAL BLACK HISTORY MONTH

FEBRUARY 11TH

**PRESIDENT OBAMA SIGNED INTO
LAW THE "CHRISTOPHER AND DANA
REEVE PARALYSIS ACT", THE FIRST
PIECE OF COMPREHENSIVE LEGISLATION
AIMED AT IMPROVING THE LIVES OF
AMERICANS LIVING WITH PARALYSIS
&
THE PRESIDENT ISSUED AN EXECUTIVE
ORDER REPEALING THE RESTRICTIONS
OF EMBRYONIC STEM CELL RESEARCH**

FEBRUARY 12TH

REFLECTIONS AT HOME
EXODUS 4: 1-17

<u>WHAT ARE YOU AFRAID OF?</u>

To receive a passing grade on an exam, there is a certain level of expectation that one studied. Not so with the current Republican field of candidates. The total lack of knowledge in regards to American History, Geography, and International Affairs of these people who want to be leaders of the United States is frightening. When I had students who obviously had not even bothered to study for an exam they knew was going to be given, it not only assured them of receiving a low or failing grade, but it showed me something about their character. Those who are excited by the absolute ignorant while swimming in the sea of mediocrity are also showing the world how America now worships at the foot of hand-gesturing fools and bravado.

When Moses was given the task of talking to the people and Pharaoh, he was afraid that no one would listen to him due to his "slow of speech." Many times, fear is born out of a feeling of inadequacy or the smiling mask of bravado. Is that why we see Michael Steele and "If I may say so" Zuckerman defending the slicing and dicing of tapes by Romney and presenting the hybrid ad as something that was said by the President? Is this how you raise your children? It's okay because everyone does it, and even though President Obama was misquoted, the meaning is real. This is exactly what is meant when as Christians, we are to be in the world, but not of the world. I am reminded of something I kept on the wall in my classroom by

Frederick Douglass known as the "Principles of Success", and perhaps it can remind all of us what is important in a candidate. No matter which party one affiliates with, the race should be run with dignity, respect, knowledge and honesty and the person who best represents you should receive your vote. "It has nothing to do with self-preservation. It has to do with right and wrong, and something called integrity."

from *True Blue* by David Baldacci

If you like sci-fi, grab some popcorn and watch the movie about the clever rat from the past. It's called "Willard".

Frederick Douglass' Principles of Success

- Understanding that the proper use of power is to help others.
- Giving up something you want in order to help someone else.
- Learning how to challenge and overcome doubt.
- Understanding why and how to control the human ego.
- Doing what is right and proper without delay, even if no one is looking.
- Learning how to use knowledge and understanding wisely.
- Overcoming indecisiveness by developing p roper organizational skills.
- Making gratitude a part of every thought and action.
- Practicing the skill of listening before making judgements.
- Remaining true to your word.
- Practicing the art of giving without expecting something in return.
- Recognizing that success is as much a motivation to others as to you.

"Moses Coming Down From Mt. Sinai" *by Gustave Doré*

Doré Bible Illustrations
• Free to Copy www.
creationism.org/images/

Exo 32:15 And Moses turned, and went down from the mount, and the two tables of the testimony were in his hand: the tables *were* written on both their sides; on the one side and on the other *were* they written.

NATIONAL BLACK HISTORY MONTH

FEBRUARY 12TH

**PRESIDENT OBAMA INITIATED
"RACE TO THE TOP" EARLY LEARNING
CHALLENGE FUND OF $500 MILLION
TO STATES THAT SHOW QUALITY
LEARNING PROGRAMS FOR VULNERABLE
CHILDREN. ON DECEMBER 16, 2011,
NINE STATES RECEIVED FUNDING.**

FEBRUARY 13TH

REFLECTIONS AT HOME
GENESIS 47: 1-12

"AFFIRMATIVE ACTION"

There was a famine in Canaan and we just had to get out. It's a good thing that we have Joseph in the family to help us. What about everybody else? What about those whose fathers or brother were not rich and famous? I like to watch Mika Brzezinski, whose father was a former National Security Advisor. I like to watch Luke Russert, whose father was the former moderator of "Meet the Press". I like to watch Willie Geist, whose father Bill is still on television. Would they have gotten their jobs without the name recognition of their parents?

Joseph not only provided nourishment to his brethren, but he placed them in Goshen, the best land of Rameses, where they and their sheep could flourish. One's faithfulness can affect the whole family. It is our duty as parents to position our children for success as much as possible. When I used to hear parent after parent say "When he's eighteen, he's on his own", or children in high school having to pay "rent" for living in the home, I couldn't sleep at night. Often they had no college fund or savings account. We had to fight to get many of the parents to even fill out the FAFSA form so the child could receive money for college. Most children unlike Mika, Luke, and Willie will not have the "affirmative action" of their parents to insure the success of their offspring. Being qualified for a job does not mean that you will get the job. Name recognition will trump most of the time.

When your children are born, or even if you are a single person, look into some form of financial planning such as *www.ingramfinancialmanagement.com*. Too often, children are seen as burdens and not as gifts from God. Do what is right. And then, train your children to do what is right by exposing them to opportunities to care for someone or something other than themselves. Pack up the car and make plans to attend the Apollo Beach Manatee Festival of the Arts in March held in Florida each year. They even have an artist competition to display one's talent. You will have fun learning about and seeing the manatee migration. Research *www.apollobeachchamber.com/manatee.htm*. Every child needs to participate in wholesome family activities. Make them put the electronics away and enjoy each other. Be affirmative when it comes to helping your children succeed. You may need them down the road, and around the corner.

"Jacob Goeth Into Egypt" *by Gustave Doré*

Gen 46:5 . . . and the sons of Israel carried Jacob their father, and their little ones, and their wives, in the wagons which Pharaoh had sent to carry him.

NATIONAL BLACK HISTORY MONTH

FEBRUARY 13TH

PRESIDENT OBAMA AND THE FIRST'
LADY ARE COMMITTED TO ENSURING
THAT CHILDREN HAVE NUTRITIOUS
MEALS TO EAT AT HOME AND AT
SCHOOL. THE COMPREHENSIVE
INITIATIVE, "LET'S MOVE", LAUNCHED
BY THE FIRST LADY IS DEDICATED TO
SOLVING THE CHALLENGE OF
CHILDHOOD OBESITY WITHIN A
GENERATION.

FEBRUARY 14TH

REFLECTIONS AT HOME
ECCLESIASTES 9: 1-12

THE GIFT OF LOVE

Are you one of the lucky ones to have married someone who still makes your heart skip a beat when he walks into the room?

The verse begins with telling us that everyone will eventually die so make the most out of life while you can. Life is unpredictable and tomorrow is not promised, so understand that life is a gift which should not be wasted. Go beyond looks, money, and material entities when finding a spouse. This reading is not about abusive husbands or self-centered wives. This is about those who are married and know how to show their appreciation for each other.

"Whatsoever thy hand findeth to do, do it with thy might . . ." (9: 10)

The commitment made to each other must be able to withstand outside interference whether it be from well meaning in-laws, single friends, children, work, or ex-spouses with an agenda. You must be a united front that demands the respect your marriage deserves. Keeping a marriage together must resemble a willow tree which gracefully bends in a storm, but never breaks.

"Live joyfully with the wife whom thou lovest . . ." (: 9)

Keep your marriage fun. Invent new things to do together. If you have children, plan a family weekend vacation to the shore or historic sight (not a relative's house), and then plan a vacation for the two of you. Traveling together bonds people. Your income should be divided into bills, savings, charity, and vacations. Do not expect the man to pay for everything when you work just as he does. You must think as a team. Until you can go to Istanbul or Paris, plan smaller. Pay an adult, not a teenager, once a week to have your children spend the night if possible. Many senior citizens would love the company and could use some extra cash. On your "free" night, cook something together like the Indian dish, Kedgeree (rice boiled with split peas, onions, curry, eggs, butter, flaked fish like smoked haddock, and some sultanas or white seedless grapes). On this Valentine's Day, plant a Dwarf Kieffer Pear tree in the yard to symbolize your life together or fix a plate of cold cuts along with a bottle of sparkling cider, and snuggle up on the sofa reading one of David Baldacci's novels. Once you read *The Collectors*, you will be hooked. So keep your perspective about your relationship and serve God.

"Go thy way, eat thy bread with joy, and drink thy wine with a merry heart . . ." (9: 7)

"The Marriage in Cana" *by Gustave Doré*

Doré Bible Illustrations
• Free to Copy www.
creationism.org/images/

Joh 2:5-7 His mother saith unto the servants. Whatsoever he saith unto you do it. And there were set there six waterpots of stone. . . . Jesus saith unto them, Fill the waterpots with water. And they filled them up to the brim.

60

NATIONAL BLACK HISTORY MONTH

FEBRUARY 14TH

PRESIDENT OBAMA SIGNED THE "WEAPONS SYSTEMS ACQUISITION REFORM ACT" TO STOP FRAUD AND WASTEFUL SPENDING IN THE DEFENSE PROCUREMENT AND CONTRACTING SYSTEM

FEBRUARY 15TH

REFLECTIONS AT HOME
1 SAMUEL 17: 32-57

THE DAVID PROJECT

Most people are familiar with the story of David and Goliath, and how David slew the giant, Goliath, when just a teen with a slingshot and a smooth stone. But, today I want to concentrate on King David, the man. Even as a young man, he was a man of action. Many times he made wrong choices which led to adultery, murder, and betrayal. David was not a repeat offender, so it seems as if he learned from his mistakes. Even though the Lord loved David, forgiveness does not mean that there are no consequences. To repent, there has to be a change in behavior as well as a change of heart.

As a parent, David did not raise his children with a firm hand which almost always causes problems as they become young adults. This brings me to the State Correctional Institution in Albion, PA. which sits on 290 acres. We are fortunate enough to have "job creating" millionaire Senator James Risch (R) of Idaho who has a degree in Forestry. The Senator has a lot to be thankful for and perhaps he is willing to share his "luck" with others not as politically connected as he. When Risch lost the 1994 primary election for state senator to Roger Madsen, Governor Phil Batt (R) named Madsen director of the commerce department, and re-appointed Risch back to the senate in 1995.

The David Project would be a complex to train carpentry to appointed men in SCI as well as teach the economic and environmental value of forests. This skill would enable the inmates to be self-employed when released and perhaps become future employers. With the expertise of Senator Risch and his network of friends, the David Project could plant and harvest trees, and then turn hardboard into cabinets, furniture, containers, paneling and signs. The men selected for this program would receive minimum wage into their release account. Companies such as Boise Cascade Corporation in Idaho and Scott Paper Company in Pennsylvania could also lend their time, talent, and treasure. In this 1,000 cell institution, we can change the lives for good of at least one hundred of them that are the least violent. On completion, each man would receive a small golden harp on a chain.

With God's help, nothing is impossible. (48)

"David and Goliath" *by Gustave Doré*

Doré Bible Illustrations
• Free to Copy www.
creationism.org/images/

1Sa 17:50 So David prevailed
over the Philistine with a sling
and with a stone, and smote the
Philistine, and slew him: but
there was no sword in the hand
of David.

NATIONAL BLACK HISTORY MONTH

FEBRUARY 15TH

PRESIDENT OBAMA COMPLETED FREE-TRADE AGREEMENTS WITH KOREA, COLUMBIA AND PANAMA WHICH WILL SUPPORT U.S. JOBS

FEBRUARY 16TH

REFLECTIONS AT HOME
GENESIS 11: 1-9

THE TOWER OF BABEL: THE SCHEIE EYE INSTITUTE

When we hear the rhetoric today of how "they" are taking away jobs from the "true" Americans, one usually thinks of migrant workers and other low-paying occupations. The Scheie Eye Institute of the University of Pennsylvania is a leader in the field of ophthalmology and their full time residency program which consists of fifteen residents and eight fellows is training the future leaders in eye care. However, if you look at the current newsletter boasting about the new rotation of candidates selected, you will see the following: J. Jun; S. Padmanabhan; M. Zaveri; D. Gewaily; L. Hariharan; A. & D. Shah; K. Eftekhari; D. Ghodasra; M. Levin; T. Choi; Y. Shayesteh; J. Abbasian; and C. Choe to name a few.

These candidates are probably all deserving of this opportunity, but when I see the African American unemployment rate which is usually double the nation's unemployment rate, it brings to mind the old saying, "We couldn't find any qualified". Perhaps this is true. So when your children of any race are not sure what they would like to pursue as a career choice, suggest that they look into the following choices:

Neuro-Opthalmology   Pediataric Opthalmalogy
Oculoplastics   Vitreoretinal Surgery

When the descendants of Noah built the ziggurat known as The Tower of Babel, using man-made brick instead of stone, it stood as a monument to the danger of arrogant people who praise themselves. They spoke the same language at the beginning, but the Lord eventually confused their language due to pride. Progress stops when there is no communication. It's no longer acceptable that you have a "few" Blacks on the job or a "few" women (who are still the majority population). If your child is in high school, send for information and the application for The University of Maryland School of Medicine: Ophthalmology and Visual Sciences. Ninth and tenth graders should concentrate on a high GPA. Take the SAT exam in May of their junior year in high school and again in December of their senior year. Mail the completed college applications (5) in September of their senior year. Let them know that they are taking the SAT again in December to achieve a higher score. Parents complete the FAFSA info in January of their senior year. Don't wait. Maybe one day we will see their names in the university newsletter.

"The Confusion of Tongues" *by Gustave Doré*

Doré Bible Illustrations
• Free to Copy www.
creationism.org/images/

Gen 11:6-8 . . . Behold, the people *is* one, and they have all one language; . . . let us go down, and there confound their language, . . . So the Lord scattered them abroad . . . .

NATIONAL BLACK HISTORY

FEBRUARY 16TH

PRESIDENT OBAMA KEPT HIS PROMISE
TO END THE WAR IN IRAQ
&
BUILT AN INTERNATIONAL COALITION
TO STOP A MASSACRE IN LIBYA AND
SUPPORTED THE LIBYAN PEOPLE AS
THEY OVERTHREW THE REGIME OF
MOAMMAR QADHAFI

FEBRUARY 17TH

REFLECTIONS AT HOME
GENESIS 4: 1-16

THE SECOND SELF

What things have you done in your past out of jealous anger? In today's reading, Cain's so-called sacrifice is rejected by God. We are not told why it was rejected because that is not important. What's important is how Cain handled the rejection. Those who refuse to admit their mistakes quite often wound up living in an isolated state of existence. Because they refuse to see their own offensive actions, they do not feel it necessary to try again, nor do they feel it necessary to apologize. Have you treated someone verbally and/or physically shameful that maybe no one even knows about but you and the one you mistreated? Did you apologize to that individual or did you take the cowardly way out and just tell others how sorry you were to have done what you did?

God placed a mark on Cain so that everyone would know who he was and the fact that he was not to be killed in retaliation for killing his brother, Abel. Instead, Cain was sentenced to be a fugitive and vagabond for life. Today, you may know some people who should wear warning signs around their necks. Warning: he is a liar and fornicator. Warning: she is self-centered and a thief. Their traits always come out eventually.

Ancient Egyptians believed that a man's "ka" or soul would inhabit a statue made to look like him in case his body was destroyed and in the next life he would be given another chance to get it right. Cain was

70

given a second chance, but chose not to use it. The Bible tells us that repentance must be shown not only in speech, but must exhibit a change in behavior.

How many people would be pleasantly surprised to receive a hand-written note of apology or a "thinking of you" card from you? What a lovely way to spend a dreary Saturday afternoon. Jealousy and anger have a way of dissipating with time. Some of that is due to maturity. Some of that is due to proximity. There is a style of writing called "flashback". This happens when the present is interrupted to show what took place in the past. Take control and do not let an unpleasant past catch up with you. Mend your bridges now.

Their Eyes Were Watching God written in 1937 by Zora N. Hurston was written in flashback style. Add this to your child's bedroom library.

"The Death of Abel" *by Gustave Doré*

Doré Bible Illustrations
• Free to Copy www.
creationism.org/images/

Gen 4:8-9 . . . Cain rose up against Abel his brother, and slew him. And the Lord said unto Cain, Where *is* Abel thy brother? And he said, I know not: *Am* I my brother's keeper?

NATIONAL BLACK HISTORY MONTH

FEBRUARY 17TH

PRESIDENT OBAMA SIGNED THE "AMERICAN RECOVERY AND REINVESTMENT ACT" WHICH PROVIDES AN EXTRA $250 PAYMENT TO SOCIAL SECURITY AND NEW RESOURCES FOR "TANF" (TEMPORARY ASSISTANCE FOR NEEDY FAMILIES) & INCREASES JOB TRAINING FUNDS BY $3.95 BILLION FOR WORKFORCE INVESTMENT WHICH SUPPORTS GREEN JOB TRAINING & SUMMER JOBS FOR YOUNG PEOPLE

FEBRUARY 18TH

REFLECTIONS AT HOME
DEUTERONOMY 23: 1-8

MAN-MADE LAWS

"HE THAT IS WOUNDED IN THE STONES, OR HATH HIS PRIVY MEMBER CUT OFF, SHALL NOT ENTER INTO THE CONGREGATION OF THE LORD". (Verse 1)

When State Rep. Dennis Baxley from Florida sponsored the "new" voting laws in time for the 2012 election, he reminded me of these verses. This reading has many titles. Some Bibles say "Those Excluded From the Congregation" and some say "Those Who Cannot Become One of the Lord's People". But this fine, upstanding member of the Baptist church knows about emasculation. Figuratively speaking, to emasculate means to destroy the force of something.

Representative Baxley (age 59) had no concerns regarding voter fraud and hanging chads when Bush stole the election, but now he is on a fake crusade to prevent voter fraud that may happen. He's denied registering on Sundays (when many Blacks do "soul to poll"), and he's changed the pre-registration rules just to name a few. Baxley, in the name of justice, has tried to emasculate the minority vote. He has decided who is qualified to "enter into the assembly".

This informed individual also sponsored an amendment in May 2011 to "give the public a voice on ending public funding of abortion".

Someone should give him a copy of the Hyde Amendment that Congress passed in 1977 which banned Medicaid coverage of abortion. It's good that Baxley likes to acknowledge his love of Gospel music, but I would like to suggest some Negro Spirituals be added to his Christian musical library. His sudden concern for voting rights comes across for exactly what it is . . .

Representative Baxley has a degree in funeral services, but he will not be able to bury the Black vote. Not this time!

"The Destruction of the Armies of the Ammonites and Moabites" *by Gustave Doré*

Doré Bible Illustrations
• Free to Copy www.
creationism.org/images/

2Ch 20:22-23 . . . the Lord set ambushments against the children of Ammon, Moab, and mount Seir, which were come against Judah; and they were smitten. . . . every one helped to destroy another.

NATIONAL BLACK HISTORY MONTH

FEBRUARY 18TH

PRESIDENT OBAMA SIGNED THE "AMERICAN RECOVERY AND REINVESTMENT ACT" WHICH INCREASES FUNDING FOR THE COMMUNITY SERVICES BLOCK GRANT FOR 1 BILLION DOLLARS & INCREASES THE WEATHERIZATION ASSISTANCE PROGRAM BY 5 BILLION TO HELP LOW INCOME FAMILIES SAVE ON THEIR ENERGY BILLS

CONRADIAN

CHARATERISTIC OF THE ISOLATED HERO WHO FINDS REDEMPTION THROUGH INVOLVEMENT

FEBRUARY 19th

REFLECTIONS AT HOME
DEUTERONOMY 7: 16-20

SANS (WITHOUT) PITY

What is it like to cause or to see the suffering of another and feel no compassion? Deuteronomy is made up of sermons given to the people by Moses while they were living in the desert. There is a distinction in the laws made by man and the teachings of Christ. Moses tells the people to destroy other nations and their false gods. The human soul and spirit are tested throughout our lifetime, and many pastors of today totally ignore preaching about the nature of evil and our very real character flaws. Ironically, the church as well as "psychology 101" should inspire discussion of this twist of human nature.

If you have gone to high school in the past fifty years, you probably had to read *Heart of Darkness* by Joseph Conrad. He was a master at conveying isolation, self-deprecation and loneliness. This was partially done by his nautical settings in many of his books. The setting is basically where and when a story takes place, however it also should include the weather; time of day; what period in time (past, present, future); people's customs or how they live, dress, and what they eat. In other words, the setting of a story should give the reader clues as to how the characters (and often the author) think.

In the study of human nature, isolation whether it be on ships sailing the oceans or in a desert like Moses, evil easily seeps into the soul. Born in 1857 to Polish parents, Conrad was an orphan by age eleven, losing his mother, Ewelina, to tuberculosis. At age sixteen, he began a colorful career as a seaman. Oddly, my teachers never discussed Conrad's "magnificient obsession" with people of color. One should always look beyond he time-honored curriculum. Find a new and different perspective. This series is designed to be a catalyst for research and discovery. It is very hard to get students to stay focused between Thanksgiving and Christmas, so plan a "Joseph Conrad" film festival the first week of December. You can even serve birthday cake as well as popcorn.

Load up the DVD with "Heart of Darkness", "The Duellists" (in 1878 Conrad was supposedly wounded in the chest as a result of a duel), and "An Outcasts of the Islands". Then parent, or teacher and student discuss and compare/contrast the setting in each film in a five—paragraph essay with an ambiguous title. Or read and compare Conrad's depiction of the half-caste "Nina" in *Almayer's Folly* to the character of "Aissa" in *An Outcast of the Islands*.

"St. John at Patmos" *by Gustave Doré*

Rev 1:9 I John, who also am your brother, and companion in tribulation, and in the kingdom and patience of Jesus Christ, was in the isle that is called Patmos, for the word of God, and for the testimony of Jesus Christ.

THE NIGGER OF THENARCISSUS (1897)

By Joseph Conrad

* Publishers in the United States changed the title to
The Children of the Sea: A Tale of the Forecastle because they felt that no one would buy a book about a Black man.

I would only have my honors 11th and 12th grade classes read this challenging book. It is not a typical book read for pleasure, but an excellent example of the isolation of the protagonist in a Conradian novel.

*One hundred and fifteen years later, Hollywood refused to produce the movie, "Red Tails" about the Black aviators known as the Tuskegee Airmen who escorted the bomber planes of WWII and outmaneuvered Nazi fighter pilots because they felt that no one would come to see a movie about Black men.

Film producer of Star Wars, George Lucas, used his own money ($58 million) to not only produce the movie, but spent an additional $35 million to market it because he felt that the Tuskegee Airmen is an untold part of American History.

I encourage you to see it if you have not already done so.
It is magnificent.

NATIONAL BLACK HISTORY MONTH

FEBRUARY 19TH

PRESIDENT OBAMA SIGNED THE
"AMERICAN RECOVERY &
REINVESTMENT ACT" WHICH
PROVIDES FOR 2 BILLION DOLLARS
IN NEW NEIGHBORHOOD
STABILIZATION FUNDS
&
1.5 BILLION IN THE HOMELESS
PREVENTION FUNDS

FEBRUARY 20th

REFLECTIONS AT HOME
1 CHRONICLES 26: 1-19

THE GATEKEEPERS

These verses tell of the four thousand temple guards and the various jobs they were called to perform. It goes to the heart of what the word "duty" means. A duty is something that one ought to do, but not necessarily something one has to do. For Christians, I think one's duty might be taken a little further in saying it's an obligation. Following the teachings of Jesus, we are called to help in whatever way we can whenever we can.

From Ethiopia, to Indonesia, to Mexico, to Canada to right here in Akron, Pennsylvania (a borough in Lancaster County) are the Mennonites. During the Protestant Reformation, they rejected the idea of infant baptism and felt the Roman Catholic Church should not require membership at birth. This is similar to the Baptist belief that the parents have their babies blessed and promise to bring them up adhering to the Christian teachings where god-parents are also asked to help with the upbringing. Around the age of ten, the child then decides for himself to be baptized and continue to live his life according to Christian doctrine. The Anabaptist Mennonite, like Martin Luther King, believe in a non-violent approach to achieve social justice and have been persecuted for this. If you own a retail shop, check out the Fair Trade retailer Ten Thousand Villages operated by the non-profit Mennonite Central Committee. If you have some free time, research the Mennonite Disaster Service at: www.mds.mennonite.net/get-involved

This is a great way to help build character in your teenagers. Both you and your teen can donate a week. You can even select the project and location of your Christian duty.

There is another type of "duty" that is seen in cases of reporting abuse be it happening to children, who are God's gift, or to animals, God's creatures. Was there a time in your life when you did not act because you were not told to do so? Walter Spies, son of a German diplomat, was a gifted artist in the 1920's. He left Berlin and wound up in Bali where he fell in love with the culture and gamelan music. He had a lot to do with the promotion of the Hindu traditional kecak dance usually performed by males dressed in checkered sarongs. The Dutch government places Spies, a homosexual, in prison for indecent behavior in 1938. He was one of the prisoners on the ship Van Imhoff in 1942 headed for Ceylon when it was hit by a Japanese torpedo boat. Although the Dutch crew abandoned ship, the captain did not set the German prisoners free because he had not received the proper orders, leaving Spies and the other prisoners to slowly drown as the ship succumbed to their watery graves. What should he have done? What was his duty? What would you have done?

"The Rebuilding of the Temple" *by Gustave Doré*

Doré Bible Illustrations
• Free to Copy www.
creationism.org/images/

Ezr 3:11 And they sang together by course in praising and giving thanks unto the Lord; because *he is* good, for his mercy *endureth* forever toward Israel. . . . because the foundation of the house of the Lord was laid.

NATIONAL BLACK HISTORY MONTH

FEBRUARY 20TH

PRESIDENT OBAMA SIGNED THE "AMERICAN RECOVERY & REINVESTMENT ACT" WHICH PROVIDED $20 BILLION INCREASE FOR THE "SNAP" PROGRAM FORMERLY KNOWN AS FOOD STAMPS, FOOD BANKS, AND "WIC" (NUTRITIONAL PROGRAM FOR INFANTS)

FEBRUARY 21ST

REFLECTIONS AT HOME
LUKE 1: 39-56

THE WISE WOMEN

Do you remember the response to the announcement that you were pregnant? When the angel told Mary that she was pregnant (the Annunciation), she immediately "went to the hill country with haste" to visit her wise, old cousin, Elizabeth (the Visitation).

Today, there are so many pregnant teenage girls who do not have the benefit of going to a wise, older woman. More often than not, the new grandmother is only fifteen years older than the new mother which only adds to the overwhelming dysfunctional household. Even those who try their best are generally undereducated and financially stressed. Prenatal care, the needed patience to care for a baby and two parents to welcome the baby rarely exist. Sometimes I could not sleep at night because we would see young mothers curse and scream at their toddlers brought to the school daycare or the time I once saw a young mother give her toddler a slim jim and some soda for breakfast. These young mothers and grandmothers need the nurturing and the compassion of older, wiser, women. Many times, one's future is determined by one's foundation.

Sibyls were women revered by the Ancients for their alleged gift of prophecy. Michelangelo painted five of them on the ceiling of the Sistine Chapel interposed between Biblical prophets. Even though the sibyls appear to have the muscular arms of my son in-law, who is a Major in the Marines, the Libyan Sibyl seems to be the most feminine. But, I encourage you to judge for yourself. (*www.italian-renaissance-art.com/Prophets.html*). Both Mary and Elizabeth knew the missions of their sons before they were born. They understood what these infants were going to do for the world through them when Mary said that "from henceforth all generations shall call me blessed."

Is there someone with child today who needs your wisdom and strength?

The Libyan Sibyl sculpted sometime between 1861 and 1868, which resides in The Metropolitan Museum of Art (*www.metmuseum.org/Collections*), is said to be modeled after Sojourner Truth but at the same time seems to honor the sibyls of the world. She has African braids, wears the Star of David, and has a Grecian nose signifying the wisdom of women worldwide.

Juno is the goddess of women and marriage in Roman mythology. She is seen as a majestic sage. Can you be a "Juno" to some young lady who needs someone to talk to?

**The Libyan Sibyl
William Wetmore
Story (American,
Boston, Massachusetts
1819-1895
Vallombrosa)**

(**http://www.italian-renaissance-art.com/Prophets.html**

The Libyan Sibyl

NATIONAL BLACK HISTORY MONTH

FEBRUARY 21ST

**PRESIDENT OBAMA SIGNED THE
"EDWARD M. KENNEDY SERVICE
AMERICA ACT" WHICH WILL
INCREASE THE SIZE OF AMERICORPS
FROM 75,000 TO 250,000 VOLUNTEERS
BY 2017**

FEBRUARY 22ND

REFLECTIONS AT HOME
DANIEL 4: 28-37

EARTHLY KINGDOMS

When Nebuchadnezzar rebuilt Babylon, he took all of the credit. Today, he would be called a self-made man or one who had "pulled himself up by his own bootstrap." As Christians, we know that there is no such person.

I first thought of all of the institutions such as the Barclay Bank, Brown University, or the College of William & Mary (research the "Lemon Project") that directly profited from slavery. Remember the promise of 40 acres and a mule? Or were your ancestors recipients of the Armed Occupation Act of 1842 used as an incentive to populate Florida whereby 160 acres were *given* to the head of the family (up to 200,000 acres); or maybe the Homestead Act of 1862 when the government *gave* away 160 acres per family; or perhaps the Enlarged Homestead Act of 1909 which *gave* away 320 acres per family, or perhaps your family benefitted from the Stock-Raising Homestead Act of 1916 which *gave* away 640 acres per family. How dare their descendants now brag about being self-made?

To pay for his arrogance, Nebuchadnezzar was forced to live with wild animals for seven years, a far cry from his luxurious palace. He did not appreciate the fact that all he had been given was through the grace of God and he should have acknowledged such. False pride had to be replaced with penance. When Nebuchadnezzar obtained absolution for his sins, he was restored to power.

It seems that many people today do not understand the concept of doing penance. What about your family? Have you condoned expensive gifts from your children never questioning where the money came from? Do you correct the disrespectful behavior of your teenager or are you still trying to be her friend?

Most people are familiar with Mardi Gras, but I want to suggest a family activity on Shrove Tuesday (the day before Ash Wednesday). To shrive means to confess one's sin and repent. In Great Britain, Shrove Tuesday is also known as Pancake Day. Have pancakes for dinner with all of the trimmings (walnuts, banana slices, strawberries, blueberries, flavored syrups). Foods containing sugar and eggs were often given up for Lent. When done, go around the table and have each person say what he would like to improve about himself. Then, have the family go to *www.givelocally.net* and chose a family to help and remind of our risen Lord.

"Daniel" *by Gustave Doré*

Dan 2:20-21 Daniel answered and said, Blessed be the name of God forever and ever; for wisdom and might are his: And he changeth the times and the seasons; he removeth kings, and setteth up kings: . . .

NATIONAL BLACK HISTORY MONTH

FEBRUARY 22ND

PRESIDENT OBAMA SIGNED
"THE TAX RELIEF, UNEMPLOYMENT
INSURANCE REAUTHORIZATION, &
JOB CREATION ACT OF 2010":

EXTENDED MIDDLE CLASS TAX
CUTS TO PREVENT AN INCREASE
OF OVER $2,000 ON JANUARY 1
&
PROVIDED A 2% PAYROLL TAX CUT
TO 159 MILLION WORKERS
(ABOUT $1,000 TAX CUT)
&
PROVIDED UP TO $10,000 TAX
CREDIT FOR FOUR YEARS OF
COLLEGE HELPING OVER 9 MILLION
STUDENTS

FEBRUARY 23RD

REFLECTIONS AT HOME
JEREMIAH 50: 30-40

DIOP PRIDE

Yesterday we saw how pride and arrogance can destroy a king. In Jeremiah, the people are warned again not to become too self-sufficient or they will be made to stumble and perish as well.

State Superintendent, John Huppenthal, of the Tucson Unified School District wants to shut down certain ethnic classes because he says they only tell one side of the American story and omits the White race. Multiple that by hundreds of supervisors and curriculum directors who have not taught one day in a high school classroom or studied the subject they are judging, yet control what is taught. Had you ever heard of the 62 African American officers arrested in 1945; or the 45-member Black Cabinet of Pres. Roosevelt in your history books? All of my life, we have had to endure one-sided American History omitting most of any significant ethnic participation in this country. What hypocritical world does he live in?

Today, we learn of a different kind of pride in a French West African poet named David Diop. Diop was born to a Senegalese father and a Cameroonian mother in Bordeauz, France in 1927. Although he was raised and educated in France, he was very involved in the plight of Africans against the cruelty of French colonialism. And, just as Nebuchadnezzar rebuilt Babylon, Diop returned to Africa in the 50's to help rebuild Senegal. Although Diop was killed in an airplane crash at age thirty-three, his poetry cries out to be read aloud and teaches the mastery of oral expression. Read the following poem, and then write an essay about what you feel he is saying. What does he mean by "The bitter taste of liberty"? How does he use the rhythms of repetition? Remember when analyzing a poem, you not only tell what it means, but what literary techniques are used and to what end.

AFRICA

Africa, my Africa
Africa of proud warriors in ancestral savannahs
Africa of whom my grandmother sings
On the banks of the distant river
I have never known you
But your blood flows in my veins
Your beautiful black blood that irrigates the fields
The blood of your sweat
The sweat of your work
The work of your slavery
Africa, tell me Africa
Is this you, this back that is bent
This back that breaks
Under the weight of humiliation
This back trembling with red scars
And saying yes to the whip under the midday sun
But a grave voice answers me
Impetuous child that tree, young and strong
That tree over there
Splendidly alone amidst white and faded flowers
That is your Africa springing up anew
Springing up patiently, obstinately
Whose fruit bit by bit acquires
The bitter taste of liberty.

*This is an excellent poem to recite in a competition for the high school or college student. Read *Discourse on Colonialism* by Aime Cesaire which can be found in paperback on *www.amazon.com* to help understand the empathy of a people enslaved.

"Isaiah's Vision of the Destruction of Babylon" *by Gustave Doré*

Doré Bible Illustrations
• Free to Copy www.creationism.org/images/

Isa 13:20-21 It shall never be inhabited, neither shall it be dwelt in from generation to generation . . . But wild beasts of the desert shall lie there; and their houses shall be full of doleful creatures; . . . .

NEGRITUDE

THE TERM COINED IN THE 1930'S BY AIME CESAIRE & L. SENGHOR

THEMES: THE HARMFUL EFFECTS OF
INFERIORITY COMPLEX

THE STRENGTH OF AFRICAN
WOMEN

NOSTALGIA FOR THE BEAUTY OF
THE AFRICAN HERITAGE

THE UNIQUE BLACK EXPERIENCE
OF TODAY

FEBRUARY

REFLECTIONS AT HOME
KNOWLEDGE IS POWER

VOCABULARY ENHANCEMENT & ACTIVITIES

Unless one attends a private school, in twelveth grade the average student has to take a year of British Literature which includes The Anglo-Saxons; The Middle Ages; The Renaissance; The Restoration; The Romantic Period; and The Victorian Period. For many students and for many reasons, this curriculum written in stone, shows little relevance especially in the ethnic classroom. For students who are basically non-readers and are years behind in their reading level, this is like the kiss of death.

Children generally learn at a higher rate when then can relate to the subject at hand. So family, for those who can do the hiragasy and for those who cannot, clear the chairs in the family room and everyone get a copy of:

A Tempest: Based on Shakespeare's 'The Tempest:'
Adaptation for a Black Theatre—by Aime Cesaire
(In paperback)

LET THE FAMILY THEATER BEGIN

NATIONAL BLACK HISTORY MONTH

FEBRUARY 23RD

PRESIDENT OBAMA SUCCESSFULLY SAVED THE AUTO INDUSTRY AND THE MANY COMPANIES THAT DEPEND ON THE BUSINESS OF THE WORKERS IN SPITE OF THE PESSIMISTS

FEBRUARY 24TH

REFLECTIONS AT HOME
MALACHI 4: 1-6

THE MARSHALL PLAN

In literature, a *simile* is a comparison of two things using the words *like* or *as*.

the day of judgement is like _____

sinful people will burn up as _____

victory will shine like _____

you will jump like _____

In 1948 the Marshall Plan was an American program initiated to help rebuild Europe after WWII. It lasted for four years and helped those who lived in regions devastated by war. By removing trade barriers, it also helped to integrate Europe as well. It's visionary component instilled a sense of hope and possibility which led to tremendous growth in the communities of a vanquished people. This endeavor was named after the Secretary of State, George Marshall.

In 1992 the college transition program known as The Prophecy Club in a certain high school in a certain small city which has been devastated by unemployment, drugs, violence, high-school drop outs, and teen pregnancies was blessed by a Vice-President of a university far, far away who seemed as Elijah to us. When nearby universities would not accept students unless they could dunk a basketball or make a touchdown regardless of SAT scores, he stepped in and gave hope where there was none. This "Elijah" visited the school and met with the students teaching the expectations of not only excellent grades but the importance of morality and ethics one must have to be successful. He spoke of the nurturing aspect of the HBCU's which welcomed them, but would demand much more from them because they would have to survive in two worlds once they graduated. The importance of unity among their peers and to always put the "Prince of Peace" first in all they do, must be an integral part of their family values. Never asking anything of the administration, rarely even receiving a thank you from a parent, he gave over $500,000. in full scholarships in eight years. He knew that his actions would change the lives of not only the students, but would forever change the family dynamics bringing "hearts of the fathers to the children" and breaking barriers. So from Ms. Shawana Gray, soon to be Dr. Shawana Gray and Mr. Dwight Cass with a Master's Degree in Electrical Engineering, and on behalf of so many others, we say thank you Mr. Marshall Paul Hughes Mitchell.

"CONGRATULATIONS"
GREETING CARD #15

PERSONALIZED GREETING CARDS

BLANK ON THE INSIDE

ALL CARDS ARE IN COLOR AND MAY BE ORDERED

ONLINE BY CONTACTING *ZOFTIG2@COMCAST.NET.*

SINGLE CARDS = $2.50 PLUS TAX

BOX OF 12 (YOUR CHOICE) = $20 PLUS TAX

($5 SHIPPING FEE FOR BOX SET)

REFLECTIONS AT HOME SELECTION

Card #:

1. Japanese statue of mother & children
   (for new moms & grandmoms)
2. Baby celebration
2b. For dog lovers (added by popular demand)
3. Egyptian culture of arm painting
   (young child's party invitation)
4. Man on Hawaiian beach
   (miss you, happy anniversary)
5. Happy Father's Day
6. Japanese bridge at night bathed in pink & blue lights
7. Wooden crosses atop the Smoky Mts. of Ashville, N.C.
   (get well soon, in sympathy, praying for you)
8. Avenue of the sphinx in Egypt
   (for travel buddies)
9. Hawaiian cemetery

10. Japanese money statues
    (for monetary gifts)
11. Hawaiian god of chatter
    (happy anniversary, birthday)
11b. Pirate ship
    (happy birthday)
12. Sands of time along the Nile River
13. Wedding Congratulations
14. In Sympathy
15. Graduation Congratulations

NATIONAL BLACK HISTORY MONTH

FEBRUARY 24TH

**PRESIDENT OBAMA TOOK THE FIGHT
TO al QAEDA AND ELIMINATED NOT
ONLY OSAMA bin LADEN, BUT
TWENTY-TWO OUT OF THIRTY OTHER
KNOWN TERRORISTS**

FEBRUARY 25TH

REFLECTIONS AT HOME
ISAIAH 2: 6-9

DOUGHFACE

The verses today center around those who choose to follow sinful customs. While both Israel and Judah still worshiped false gods such as Ashtoreth, goddess of fertility, Isaiah warned them to rely on the Lord for help instead.

"They worship the work of their own hands" (2:8)

One of the most out-of-touch, disgraceful presidents of the United States was the fifteenth president, James Buchanan (the only president from Pennsylvania) from 1857-1861.

His motto was, "I acknowledge no master but the law."

Even though he felt that secession from the Union was illegal, he also felt that it was just as illegal to go to war to stop it. He was what we call today someone who always passes the buck of responsibility. When the Dred Scott Decision was passed asserting that Congress had no constitutional power to exclude slavery in the territories, to gain the admission of the territory of Kansas, he sided with the South and approved of the proslavery Lecompton Constitution (research this). Buchanan even is said to have offered cash in exchange for votes similar to the bought politicians of today by lobbyist money. He felt that Southerners had a right to own slaves. After all, in his third annual speech to the Nation, he said that "the slaves were treated with kindness and humanity."

A "doughface" is a northern person with southern principles and customs.

Newt Gingrich: wants to make poor Black children janitors in the schools they attend because they have no ethical role models like him in their neighborhoods. Yes, Newt should teach the children about ethics and honesty. The very machine he helped to create is literally kicking his rump and now he whines daily. Maybe one of those children could teach him about making a hangman's noose for someone else. DOUGHFACE.

Rick Santorum: who is going to stop giving money to all of those Black people on welfare. What about the Whites on welfare who outnumber every ethnic group getting public assistance? DOUGHFACE.

Rick Perry: and his "Nigger" rock at the summer estate. DOUGHFACE.

Ron Paul: who wants to bring back "property rights" so if a restaurant or hotel owner chooses to not serve Blacks, he legally does not have to do so. DOUGHFACE.

NATIONAL BLACK HISTORY MONTH

FEBRUARY 25TH

**PRESIDENT OBAMA PASSED THE
"HEALTH CARE REFORM ACT"
AND NOW MY SON, IN LAW SCHOOL,
CAN REMAIN ON MY INSURANCE UNTIL
HE IS 26 YEARS OLD**

**INSURANCE COMPANIES CANNOT
REFUSE YOU FOR PRE-EXISTING
CONDITIONS**

**INSURANCE COMPANIES CANNOT
CANCEL YOUR INSURANCE WHEN YOU
GET SICK**

**YOU DO NOT NEED VOUCHERS TO PAY
FOR PART OF YOUR MEDICAL BILL,
AND YOU PAY THE REST**

FEBRUARY 26TH

REFLECTIONS AT HOME
JOB 42: 1-8

"THE PROFESSOR"

Do you remember Russell Johnson from Ashley, PA? What if I said do you remember "The Professor" on the sitcom Gilligan's Island? When Russell was a child, his father died and he and his brothers were placed in the private boarding school for poor White males known as Girard College. Today, Girard College is integrated and has a visionary President, Mrs. Autumn A. Graves. After graduating from Girard College, Russell joined he United States Army Air Force where he flew forty-four combat missions and eventually was shot down in the Philippines in 1945. Breaking both of his ankles in the crash, he was awarded a Purple Heart.

In Job, we are told to avoid making judgements about people, as did the friends of Job, and to not talk about things which we really don't know because we have not walked in another's shoes. For years we watched Mr. Johnson on not only Gilligan's Island, but on Twilight Zone; Gunsmoke; Ironsides, and many more. Many probably only thought of the glamorous "Hollywood" lifestyle he led.

". . . Who is this who hides counsel without knowledge?

Therefore I have uttered what I did not understand, . . ." (42:3)

The verses also tell us that both good and evil people will suffer in life.

Then at the young age of thirty-nine, Russell's son, David, died from complications of AIDS in 1994. Job lost all of his children but the Bible tells us to resist self pity. When one's heart is breaking over the death of his child, all of the glitz and glory of Hollywood seems superfluous and so-o-o unimportant. It is very hard for a parent to sit by, helpless to save his child, and try to understand why. In the African and Middle East cultures, sorrow is expressed by "sitting in dust and ashes." When something happens of which you have no control, and your heart is broken, get a pen and some paper and just write. Spelling, grammar, sentence structure does not matter, just write. Writing is catharsis. It emotionally purifies or purges one's soul. This is for your eyes only, this is for your tears only. Write to release, repent, and allow Him to restore.

So, when someone or something is taken away, ... write.

"Job Hearing of His Ruin" *by Gustave Doré*

Doré Bible Illustrations
• Free to Copy www.
creationism.org/images/

Job 1:20-22 Then Job arose, and rent his mantle, and shaved his head, and fell down upon the ground, and worshipped. . . . the Lord gave, and the Lord hath taken away; . . . In all this Job sinned not . . .

Alfalfa Died Today

Alfalfa died today. My caramel-colored friend who I found about fifteen years ago tucked under my top step by his brave mother. On the street, male cats tend to kill the babies unless the female cat is there to protect and nurture. The mother cat had been in a fierce battle that night in the pouring rain. Her face showed the scars of motherly love as she bravely hid her babies under our top step. They were only two weeks old, so the vet told us the next day.

The caramel-colored one was identical to his mother unlike his calico sister. As a single mom raising two small children, it felt like I was just adding two more to the family. There can't be too much love around a house full of kids and kittens. I watched them grow as did my two children, Attiyya and Bashan. The first night we found them, I could hold both of them in the palm of my hand. Now they walk a little slower, and eat more as they embrace maturity.

Maybe because my children are grown and no longer living at home, I can't stop crying as yet another one leaves. But this one won't be coming anymore when I call his name.

The night before last, he kept trying to get into my lap and I wouldn't let him. When I came home from work last night I couldn't find him. My husband came home and found him in an outer room in the basement seemingly disoriented. He didn't eat. Instead, he walked into his carrier (which he never goes near), looked at me and laid down.

I washed his sheet and dried it with Bounce scented sheets, folded it to make it fluffy and placed it on the floor in front of the carrier. He slowly got up and walked out and laid down on the sheet but only for a few minutes as if to say "thank you". He then got up and walked back inside his carrier. The next morning he was still in the carrier so we took him to the University of Pennsylvania Animal Hospital.

They didn't think that he would live through the operation which would cost between six to eight thousand dollars. We stroked his head, took his picture, and we walked to the car in disbelief.

When I receive his ashes, I'll bury them under a rose bush and remember how he used to "help" me at Easter time. But today all I can do is cry.

My Alfalfa died today. My baby died today. My friend died today.

SAYING GOODBYE

NATIONAL BLACK HISTORY MONTH

FEBRUARY 26TH

**PRESIDENT OBAMA LAUNCHED THE
"ADVANCED MANUFACTURING
PARTNERSHIP (AMP)":
$300M FOR DOMESTIC
MANUFACTURING CAPABILITIES
$100M IN RESEARCH
$70M IN ROBOTICS RESEARCH
$120M IN ENERGY EFFICIENT
MANUFACTURING**

FEBRUARY 27TH

REFLECTIONS AT HOME
JOHN 5: 31-40

THE WITNESS

Do you know someone who always brags about how much money she makes, yet never has twenty dollars to her name? Or, someone who goes on and on about how he was not born and raised in "the ghetto", yet has had some nefarious dealings in his past with the law? In John 5, we are told that you cannot be your own witness. Such people are legends in their own minds and the truth is not in them. When one writes a characterization of a person, one of the things which must be included is how other people see this person. Thus, John the Baptist served as the witness for the coming of Christ. John is referred to as a "burning, and shining lamp" but only for a time. His light had to diminish so that Jesus, the true light, could shine. Unfortunately, some pastors and priests seem to have forgotten their mission. The egocentristic view of themselves have ruined many churches and parishes. Too many have become as the Pharisees—so caught up in their power and their rules, they have missed the Savior.

Continuing the "fine arts" theme this month, I want to honor another witness for the glory of the Lord in the personage of Marian Anderson, born February 27, 1897. While the European opera companies were offering her contracts to perform, the Daughters of the American Revolution (DAR) organization was perpetuating its racist agenda in the

United States by refusing to allow Ms. Anderson, an African-American contralto, to sing in Constitution Hall. As part of your personal musical library, treat yourself and buy a CD of her rendition of Negro Spirituals. She is a true witness to the power of an awesome God.

Jesus can also select His own witness to magnify His teachings no matter what some parents have taught. Babies are not born as racists. They are taught. In his infinite wisdom to turn what was meant for evil into good, He chose an angel in the First Lady Eleanor Roosevelt who changed the venue to an open-air concert on Easter Sunday, April 9, 1939 on the steps of the Lincoln Memorial in Washington, D.C. where Ms. Anderson sang to some 75,000 people. So, when you take your children to D.C. to show them the magnificence of the Dr. King memorial, or where our first Black president took the oath of office, be sure to go to the steps of the Lincoln Memorial to let their imagination go back in time over seventy years ago to that glorious Easter morning.

"John the Baptist Preaching in the Wilderness" *by Gustave Doré*

Doré Bible Illustrations
• Free to Copy www.
creationism.org/images/

Mar 1:6-7 And John was clothed with camel's hair, and with a girdle of a skin about his loins; and he did eat locusts and wild honey; And preached, saying, there cometh one mightier than I after me, ...

NATIONAL BLACK HISTORY MONTH

FEBRUARY 27TH

**PRESIDENT OBAMA SIGNED THE
"AMERICAN RECOVEREY AND
REINVESTMENT ACT (ARRA)"
WHICH PROVIDES FUNDS TO HIRE
& TRAIN 1,500 TEMPORARY CLAIMS
PROCESSORS TO SPEED BENEFITS
&
IMPROVE MEDICAL FACILITIES AND
CONSTRUCT STATE NURSING HOMES
FOR VETS**

FEBRUARY 28TH

REFLECTIONS AT HOME
EXODUS 6: 28-30

WHO OR WHAT SPEAKS FOR YOU?

"And Moses said before the Lord, "Behold, I am of uncircumcised lips, and how shall Pharoah hearken unto me?" (Verse 30)

There are many ways to tell the world who you are. If you wore a military cap with a round, flat top and a visor called a *kepi*, you were probably a soldier in the Civil War. If you wear a small cap, known as a *juliet*, with mesh or lace especially used to support a wedding veil, one would assume that you are a bride.

Their attire speaks for them.

Following the teachings of Amos for the rich to help those in need, Denzel Washington donated 2.25 million to his alma mater, Fordham University as did Ray Charles, so impressed with the Wilberforce University Choir under the direction of Mr. Jeremy Winston, that he left the choir 2 million dollars in his will. And, after six generations of a Republican dynasty, the great-grandson of the oil tycoon, John D. Rockefeller, known as Jay Rockefeller, the Democratic Senator of West Virginia helped advance the $30 million state-of-the-art Blanchette

Rockefeller Neurosciences Institute research facility at West Virginia University in 2008.

Their hearts spoke for them

For some unknown reason, many times during my career as a teacher, children who could not express themselves in writing or oratorically, were gifted in art. Introduce your high school student to the life and art of Rosa Bonheur who was born in Bordeaux, France in 1822. She was expelled form many schools because of her disruptive behavior, yet it was her mother who discovered Rosa's love of animals and used this as a means for Rosa to express herself. One of her most famous paintings of animals is *Horse Fair*, completed in 1855. It measures eight feet high and sixteen feet wide.

Their art speaks for them.

In the reading of February 12th, in Exodus 4:10, we learned that Moses is "slow of speech and slow of tongue" which indicated that perhaps he stuttered or he was not able to gather his thoughts in a timely manner, but here Moses talks about "uncircumcised lips". Figuratively, to circumcise means to cleanse of sin. Did Moses feel unworthy because he killed an Egyptian while defending a Hebrew slave? Moses was quick to react in many ways. Why else may he have felt unclean?

Aaron spoke for him.

Let your children know that many people have imperfections and that they can overcome them. Enhance this discussion topic by watching the movie, "The King's Speech" starring Colin Firth. So, pass the buttered popcorn and enjoy.

"Moses and Aaron Before Pharoah" *by Gustave Doré*

Doré Bible Illustrations
• Free to Copy www. creationism.org/images/

Exo 7:10 And Moses and Aaron went in unto Pharaoh, . . . and Aaron cast down his rod before Pharaoh, and before his servants, and it became a serpent.

NATIONAL BLACK HISTORY MONTH

FEBRUARY 28th

PRESIDENT OBAMA SIGNED THE
"VOW TO HIRE HEROES ACT"
INTO LAW WHICH PROVIDES TAX
CREDIT TO BUSINESSES THAT
HIRE UNEMPLOYED VETERANS
A MAXIMUM CREDIT OF $5,600
PER VETERAN
&
OFFERS BUSINESSES THAT HIRE
VETERANS WITH SERVICE-CONNECTED
DISABILITIES A MAXIMUM CREDIT
OF $9,600 PER VETERAN

NOVEMBER 21, 2011

FEBRUARY 29TH

REFLECTIONS AT HOME
ROMANS 12: 9-21

THREE SISTERS HARVEST

Community means all the people living in the same place AND subject to the same laws. Unfortunately in this country, the latter is seldom true. In Romans 12, we are told to love our community and that Christian hospitality is best shown by sharing a meal together. A good time to do this is after Sunday service or once a month with a few friends in your home. Love requires work and declares that we are to take care of each other.

Eli, a high priest and judge of Israel failed to discipline and correct his wayward sons. The sons of William Penn is said to have swindled the Lenape Indians out of their land, known as *The Walking Purchase*, before the British placed bounties on the heads of the Native Americans. In 1758, the U.S. government forced the Lenape from their homelands in Pennsylvania and New Jersey.

You and your family can make a difference in God's community of caring. When children go to Allentown, PA, it's usually to the bit amusement park, but this time make plans to visit the Museum of Indian Culture on Fish Hatchery Road. In August, they have the "Roasting Ears of Corn Festival". Share a meal of Kiowa fry bread and other ethnic foods. Three Sisters Harvest is the name of the food assistance program which serves Indian families in Pennsylvania, New Jersey, and New York so when you visit, first look at the website and bring a food item from their list: *www.museumofindianculture.org*

I have included the donation suggestions for those who do not have internet service and would still like to donate. There is a term called "Job's comforter". This is a person who increases the misery of the people he is pretending to comfort. These verses which tell us to behave as Christmas, warn us not to pretend to care, and do nothing.

Daily life can be unbearable when you and your family live in a run-down poorly insulated trailer, your food is being cooked on a hotplate, and the only running water is outside. The Museum of Indiana Culture has located federally recognized American Indian families who live in these conditions right here in the Northeast.

Over the past 5 years, Three Sisters Harvest, the Museum of Indian Culture's food assistance program, has been disbursing food to American Indian families living in Pennsylvania, New Jersey, and New York. Currently there are more impoverished American Indians who not only need food assistance, but have a difficult time without it.

In today's challenging economy, Three Sisters Harvest donations have been disappointing. Consequently, we have not been able to meet the basic needs of those so desperately needing help. *Please consider making a donation today.* Even a $10 donation or a bag of rice can make a difference.

The following Food and Misc. items are recommended:

Canned Meats:
Chicken, Tuna, Corned Beef, Ham

Canned Soups, Stews, Pastas
Cream of Broccoli Soup
Cream of Chicken Soup
Tomato and Chicken Soup
Beef Stew, Chili, Ravioli

Baking Needs
Flour, Corn Meal, Yeast
Instant Biscuit Mix, Canola Oil
Baking Powder, Baking Soda
Salt & Pepper, Chili Powder
Cinnamon, Sugar

Pasta Products
Spaghetti, Elbow Macaroni,
Macaroni and Cheese

Fruits / Vegetables
Variety of Canned Fruit
Variety of Canned Vegetables
Canned Potatoes / Sweet Potatoes
Dried Fruits and Vegetables

Canned Tomato Products
Tomato Sauce, Spaghetti Sauce,
Stewed Tomatoes

Beans:
Canned and Dried
Kidney, Pinto, Navy Beans

Cereal

Wal-Mart Gift Cards
To purchase much needed fresh meats, fruits, and vegetables

You can drop off your donations during the Museum's regular business hours Friday through Sunday, from 12 Noon to 4 pm, or during any of our yearly Festivals or special events.

If you prefer to make a monetary donation please make your check payable to Museum of Indian Culture. Three Sisters Harvest and mail to:

Museum of Indian Culture
2825 Fish Hatchery Road
Allentown, PA 18103.

Wal-Mart gift cards should also be mailed to the above address.

Only with your help can we lessen the burden for impoverished federally recognized American Indian families by making your generous donation today.

Variety of Boxed Breakfast Cereals, Oatmeal

Miscellaneous
Bags of Rice, Instant Mashed Potatoes
Nuts, Peanut Butter, Jelly / Jam
Grated Parmesan Cheese
Apple, Grapefruit, or Grape Juice
Coffee and Tea
Powdered Milk, Evaporated Milk

Paper / Cleaning Products
Toilet Paper
Sanitary Napkins
Toothpaste
Moisturizer
Laundry Soap, Bleach
Ivory Soap
Shampoo & Conditioner

The Museum of Indian Culture was founded in 1980 and is a member-supported non-profit organization registered with the Pennsylvania Bureau of Charitable Organizations. All donations are tax deductible to the extent allowed by law.

NATIONAL BLACK HISTORY MONTH

FEBRUARY 29TH

PRESIDENT OBAMA SIGNED THE "CLAIMS RESOLUTION ACT OF 2010" PROVIDING FUNDING FOR THE SETTLEMENT AGREEMENTS IN THE COBELL LAWSUIT BENEFITTING NATIVE AMERICANS & THE PIGFORD II LAWSUIT BENEFITTING AFRICAN AMERICAN FARMERS

UNITY AND DIVERSITY
ACCORDING TO HIS WORD

People fear what they do not know. So, if you are thinking of buying a summer or permanent home in Florida, do not only think of Miami Beach. The good people of Anna Maria would welcome a much more diverse community than what it currently has today. Although they "oppose" big government and will tell you that the "stimulus" was a failure, the FEDERAL TRANSPORTATION ENHANCEMENT GRANT PROGRAM gave the Anna Maria officials $859,000 so they could build an 850 ft. long boardwalk with turtle-friendly lighting; benches; 2 shelters; a trolley stop; landscaping; new pier sign and a redesigned parking lot. If the beach is not your thing, then Alford and Altha, Florida communities look forward to becoming more diverse. Heck, even the manatees of Apollo Beach will give you a warm welcome.

FEBRUARY

REFLECTIONS AT HOME
KNOWLEDGE IS POWER

Vocabulary Enhancement & Activities

HIRAGASY-a day-long musical tradition in Madagascar, especially in the Highland regions, of a mixture of opera, dancing & acting Welcome the month of February at your church or school by performing a hiragasy adhering to the correct structure & costumes. Assign people in two groups of twelve and a dedicated leader for each group for the competition (Groups alternate each part before moving to the next one)

Part 1: The Sasitehaka (10 minutes)

Drummers beat out a military rhythm with males only seated

Part 2: The Mpikabary

Male in group removes his straw hat and invites females of the group on stage where they do a dance. Male then introduces the theme of the show in a poem.

Part 3: The Renihira

Group forms a circle facing outward and sing in harmony using hand gestures and facial expressions

Part 4: The Dihy (theme-related dances)

Dance 1—style should be acrobatic or inspired from martial arts

Dance 2—performed by a male dancer

Part 5: The Zanakira
The final dance of the entire group
(Always select an odd number for the judges to avoid a tie, or allow the
audience to vote if possible)

* * *

Design invitations: Illustrate the great red island (because of the soil) with large gnarled trees thought to ensure the protection of dead ancestors

* * *

Public Relations: Invite the city zoo to bring some of its lemurs, which means ghost in Latin, as part of the Madagascar landscape

* * *

Food: Get an African cookbook. Use the culminating dinner as a fund raiser.
Be sure to have plenty of shredded beef, rice, and greens.

"WHAT I NOW KNOW"

1. In what state were 162 African American Air Force officers arrested?

    _____

    Why? _____

2. Who was Matthias W. Baldwin?

    _____

3. Name 2 mandates of the Nazarite vow of service.

    _____

    _____

4. What are "crystal tresses"?

    _____

5   What was the name of Hannah's husband?

    _____

6. How many charities are mentioned in this book? _____

Name one you can help. _____

7. What was the Marshall Plan of 1948?

    _____